Recipes from a Maple Queen

Doreen Lyon

To my parents,
Theresa & Richard

7

17

24

42

51

78

Contents

Acknowledgements

A few years ago, I started thinking about creating a maple recipe cookbook. Over this last year, the book finally started taking shape. There was a lot of making recipes, taking photos, and taste-testing by family. Special thanks to my family and friends for their support and critiques, especially my son, Jared, for helping with design, organization, and making this book possible.

When I won the title of Vermont Maple Queen in 1970, besides a tiara and sash, I also received a handmade silver maple leaf pin. This beautiful pin, which is featured on the cover of this book, was designed and made by Luella Schroeder at The Craft Shop at Molly's Pond in East Cabot, VT. I've always cherished it and consider it one of my favorite pieces.

Being a Vermont native, I use only syrup produced locally. In fact, I don't think I've ever used syrup produced out of state. I'm very thankful to have both family and friends who are maple syrup producers. The syrup used in these recipes was provided by:

Taylor Sugarwoods
Francis & Helene Taylor
334 Barton-Orleans Rd
Barton, VT 05822
802-525-3456

Red Roof Maple Works
Stan & Rhoda Weed
2529 North Ridge Rd
Sutton, VT 05867
802-427-3357

Every Vermont maple syrup producer is required to grade its syrup. One of the easiest ways to do that is to purchase a Vermont Maple Syrup Grading Kit yearly. The grading kit featured in this book, as well as the lollipop molds used for the *Maple Lollipops* (page 80), were purchased from Leader Evaporator Co., Inc. (leaderevaporator.com).

One of my favorite baking stores, which is also a bakery and offers baking classes, is King Arthur Flour in Norwich, VT. You will notice a few of my recipes use an ingredient called "natural maple flavoring." I sometimes use this in addition to the syrup to enhance the maple flavor. The flavoring is made from the end-of-season syrup called "black strap," which has the strongest maple flavor. I always purchase this flavoring, called Boyajian Natural Maple Flavor, from King Arthur Flour (kingarthurflour.com).

Finally, thanks to you, the reader. Keep in touch and join the conversation at my website: **recipesfromamaplequeen.com**.

Above: The Taylor family sugar house in 2011.
Bottom: Dad gathering, transferring, and boiling sap at the Vance sugar house (my first) in 1958.
Opposite page, top: Sitting on the sugar house steps (front left) with my siblings in 1958.
Opposite page, bottom: Celebrating my Maple Queen win wearing the tiara, sash, and pin in 1970.

Introduction

Growing up with Maple

One might be surprised to learn that, for such a small state, Vermont produces more maple syrup than any other state: half a million to a million gallons annually. Being a native Vermonter, I've found that maple syrup production has been an important part of my life beginning at a very young age. I have vivid memories and recollections from my first sugar house. It was in the late 50s, and my dad gathered sap with horses. I remember how he gave commands to move them ahead where he was waiting to dump the sap into the gathering tank they were pulling. The sap would then be transferred to tanks at the sugar house where it would be boiled into syrup. Later, we moved to the current

homestead, and my parents bought the adjoining property, which included the sugar house and bush. My siblings and I spent many childhood years helping with the spring sugaring operation. Generations of my family look forward to the spring and visiting the sugar house. Recently, my brother and his wife bought the sugar house and bush from our parents, guaranteeing it will continue to produce syrup for many years to come.

Becoming a Maple Queen

Having been a part of my family's maple production, I decided at 16 to enter the Vermont Maple Queen competition. The competition was held in January at the auditorium in Barre, during the annual, three-day Vermont Farm Show. We were judged on our knowledge of maple production, oratory skills, and poise. There were 18 contestants; I didn't think I had a chance of winning. So it was a great surprise when I was announced as the new 1970 Vermont State Maple Queen. I can still see the look of pride on my parents' faces.

Thus began a year of participating in various events across the state and New England. In March, I served

sugar on snow to the Governor and legislators at the State Legislative "Sugar on Snow" Party. In April, I rode in the Governor's Parade at the St. Albans Maple Festival. That same month I appeared on the WCAX-TV show "Across the Fence," where I presented a program on the uses of maple syrup in cooking and made three recipes, which you will find in this book. In June, I was an honored guest at the Vermont Dairy Festival, which took place in Enosburg Falls. Finally, it was off to Massachusetts in September for the Eastern States Expo, where I served sugar on snow in the Vermont building. Those are just some of the highlights from that busy year.

Years later, in 2009 at the St. Albans Maple Festival, there was a gathering to celebrate the 50th anniversary of the Vermont Maple Queen competition. About half of the queens from over the years were present. I remember talking with coordinator Betty Carr, a woman whose lifelong commitment and dedication to the Maple Queen competition were unmatched. We were reminiscing about my 1970 competition, and she told me that she knew the minute she saw me that I was the one. She never did explain why, but she said she had me picked from the start.

Maple in Recipes

The art of maple syrup production has changed dramatically over the years from buckets to pipe lines to osmosis machines; wood-fired to oil-fired arches; manual to automatic draw-off machines. Along with changes in production, the use of maple in recipes has also changed with many new ways to use maple syrup and maple sugar in cooking.

In this book, you will find an example of the many ways maple syrup is incorporated into recipes, from appetizers to dessert. This compilation of recipes has been acquired (and in some cases slightly modified) over the many years that I've spent around maple syrup. Some are long-time family recipes; others are more recently developed.

Use the recipes in this book to prepare a special meal for family and friends. The recipes in the candy section make great gifts. Remember, the uses for maple syrup and maple sugar are limited only by your imagination. Experiment with some of your own recipes.

Enjoy, and happy cooking!

Top left (and opposite page): Meeting Governor Davis and serving Sugar on Snow in 1970.
Top right: Sap runs into one of two sap houses at the Taylor sugar house in 2002.
Right middle: Gallon and half-gallon cans wait to be filled.
Bottom: Sugaring old and new at the Taylor and Weed sugar houses in 2003.

Maple Drizzle and Granulated Maple Sugar with Vermont Maple Syrup Grading Kit (page ix)

The Basics

Maple Drizzle

2 cups maple syrup
(preferrably fancy grade)

Pour maple syrup into a pretty syrup pitcher and drizzle over fruit, vegetables, pancakes, hot cereal, ice cream, yogurt; it is also great added to coffee or milk.

A little maple syrup can enhance any dish!

Granulated Maple Sugar

YIELD: 2 cups, PREP: 5 min, COOK: 30 min

1 pint dark amber maple syrup
1 tsp. butter (for coating pot)

Butter sides of a large pot. Place syrup in pot and, using a candy thermometer, cook to 265°F. Remove from heat and whip on high speed with electric mixer. Syrup will turn thick and cloudy.

Continue whipping until granulated and dry, about 7 minutes. Reduce mixer to low speed and beat until cool. Sift into a bowl and store in air-tight container.

Vermont Maple Syrup Grades

Fancy (light amber)
Flavor: Mild, subtle maple flavor
Use: Gourmet grade, best used as a drizzle on ice cream or pancakes, allowing the subtle flavor to stand out.

Grade A Dark Amber
Flavor: Pronounced maple flavor
Use: All purpose, great for cooking and making candy.

Grade A Medium Amber
Flavor: Distinct maple flavor
Use: Table and all purpose

Grade B (dark, dark amber)
Flavor: Strong maple flavor
Use: Excellent for baking where you want a distinct maple flavor.

Maple Sugar

YIELD: 2 cups, PREP: 5 min, COOK: 50 min

2 cups dark maple syrup
1 tsp. butter (for coating pan)

Pour syrup into a large heavy saucepan and butter sides; set over high heat. Clip a candy thermometer to the side of the pan. Don't stir; stirring will cause the sugar to crystallize prematurely. Cook to 238°F and remove from heat.

Stir the mixture until it changes to a grainy consistency and becomes lighter in color, five to 10 minutes. Pour the mixture into a container and let cool.

Maple sugar in the solid form was originally made by Native Americans. It could be easily transported and stored for later use. As children we would scrape the sugar out of the container to use in recipes such as Dad's Favorite Maple Cake (page 55). Granulated maple sugar, because of its ease of use, is preferred for cooking today.

Maple Syrup as Granulated Sugar Substitute

To substitute for 1 cup of granulated white sugar:

USE: 1 cup maple syrup
Maple syrup can be substituted equally for white sugar in a recipe. Maple syrup is not as sweet as white sugar though, so use a larger amount if you like your food sweeter.

ADD: ½ teaspoon of baking soda
Maple syrup is acidic. When used in a batter, the syrup needs to be neutralized for the batter to rise properly. If your recipe contains natural neutralizers, such as sour milk, buttermilk, or sour cream, you do not need to add the baking soda.

DECREASE: another liquid in the recipe by 2 to 4 tablespoons.
Because maple syrup is a liquid, it contains more moisture than the replaced white sugar.

DECREASE: Reduce oven temperature by 25°F
The maple syrup will tend to caramelize and burn sooner than a batter using white sugar.

Sugar on Snow

YIELD: 8 servings, PREP: 10 min, COOK: 40 min

1 quart of maple syrup
1 tsp. butter (for coating pot)
Packed snow

Butter the inside top 2" of a large pot and heat syrup, watching carefully so that the syrup doesn't boil over. When a candy thermometer reaches 236°F, remove pot from heat and test by spooning a little syrup over the snow. It is ready if the syrup sits on top of the snow and clings to a fork like taffy. Pour over packed snow and enjoy.

Traditionally, Sugar on Snow is always served with Raised Doughnuts (page 25) and sour pickles. The pickles help cut the sweetness of the sugar. Not a sugar season goes by without having sugar on snow at my family's sugar house.

Cheesy Pancakes and oatmeal with Granulated Maple Sugar (page 1)

Breakfast

Cheesy Pancakes

YIELD: 9 pancakes, PREP: 10 min, COOK: 15 min

2 eggs
½ cup granulated maple sugar
1 cup milk
4 Tbsp. butter, melted
1 tsp. vanilla
2 cups flour
1 tsp. baking powder
½ tsp. salt
1 cup small curd cottage cheese

In a large bowl, beat eggs, maple sugar, milk, butter, and vanilla. Combine in a medium bowl the flour, baking powder, and salt. Add to egg mixture, mixing just until combined. Stir in cottage cheese.

Spray a griddle with cooking spray. Pour ⅓ cup of batter per pancake onto hot griddle. Cook until bubbles form on top and then flip, approximately 2½ minutes per side. Serve with pure fancy maple syrup.

Pressed for time? Add cottage cheese to a store-bought pancake mix for quick cheesy pancakes.

French Toast Bake

YIELD: 6 servings, PREP: 20 min plus overnight, BAKE: 50 min

2½ cups milk
6 eggs, beaten
¾ cup maple syrup
1 tsp. vanilla
½ tsp. cinnamon
12 slices French bread (1" thick)
¼ cup butter, melted
¼ cup granulated maple sugar
1 cup walnuts, chopped

In a large bowl, whisk together milk, eggs, maple syrup, vanilla, and cinnamon. Dip bread slices into milk mixture and arrange in a 13" x 9" lightly greased baking pan overlapping the bread slices. Pour remaining milk mixture over bread, cover, and refrigerate overnight.

In the morning, while preheating the oven, melt butter and add granulated maple sugar. Pour over the bread and sprinkle with chopped walnuts. Bake at 375°F for 50 minutes or until a knife inserted in the middle comes out clean.

Consider serving with a dusting of confectioners' sugar or a drizzle of maple syrup.

Maple Breakfast Rolls and Maple Corn Muffins (page 26) with Candied Bacon

Maple Breakfast Rolls

YIELD: 12 rolls, PREP: 20 min plus chilling, BAKE: 10 min

10 slices bacon
 1 can refrigerated crescent rolls
 3 Tbsp. soft butter
¼ cup granulated maple sugar
⅓ cup confectioners' sugar
 2 Tbsp. maple syrup

Microwave bacon on paper towel-lined plate until very crisp, about 5 minutes; set aside to cool.

Line a large cookie sheet with parchment paper. Unroll dough on a lightly floured work surface, press into 12" x 8" rectangle. Spread 2 Tbsp. of the butter evenly over dough, covering to the edges. Sprinkle maple sugar over butter.

Finely chop bacon; reserve 1 Tbsp. for garnish. Spread bacon evenly over maple sugar. Starting at the short end, roll up dough, pinching edge to seal. Wrap in plastic wrap and refrigerate for 10 minutes so dough will be easier to cut. Unwrap roll, place seam side down on cutting board. Using a sharp knife, cut into 12 ¾-inch slices.

Bake at 375°F for 10 minutes or until golden brown. Remove rolls to cooling rack and cool 5 minutes. Meanwhile, in small bowl, mix confectioners' sugar, maple syrup, and remaining 1 Tbsp. of butter until smooth. Drizzle over warm rolls and garnish with remaining bacon.

Candied Bacon

YIELD: 4 servings, PREP: 5 min, COOK: 10 min

 1 lb. bacon
½ cup maple syrup

Cook bacon in cast iron pan until done. Add maple syrup to pan and cook until bacon is coated.

Serve as an addition to your breakfast/brunch menu or as a unique appetizer.

Maple Coffee Cake with Streusel Topping

YIELD: 12 servings, PREP: 25 min, BAKE: 1 hour

1½ cups butter, softened
½ cup brown sugar, packed
7 eggs
1 Tbsp. vanilla
1½ cups maple syrup
2 tsp. baking powder
½ tsp. baking soda
½ tsp. salt
4¼ cups cake flour

In a large mixing bowl, beat butter and brown sugar. Add eggs, one at a time, beating well after each addition. Add vanilla, syrup, baking powder, baking soda, and salt. On low speed of mixer, gradually add flour and beat until smooth.

Pour half of batter into 10" greased tube pan. Prepare *Streusel Topping* (below) and sprinkle half onto batter. Pour in remaining batter and sprinkle the last of the streusel mixture on top. Bake on middle rack in oven at 350°F for 1 hour or until done. Cool in pan on rack for 15 minutes. Loosen cake and invert onto serving dish.

Streusel Topping

YIELD: 3 cups, PREP: 5 min

1¼ cups brown sugar, packed
¾ cup flour
½ cup butter, melted
2 tsp. cinnamon
1 cup walnuts, chopped

Combine all ingredients in a small bowl.

Maple Nut Scones

YIELD: 8 servings, PREP: 25 min, BAKE: 25 min

2¼ cups flour
¾ cup butter
¼ cup granulated maple sugar
1 Tbsp. baking powder
½ tsp. baking soda
¼ tsp. nutmeg
½ tsp. cinnamon
½ tsp. salt
¾ cup milk
½ tsp. natural maple flavoring*
½ cup walnuts, chopped
1 egg white, beaten
3 Tbsp. maple syrup
⅓ cup confectioners' sugar

*Refer to page ix.

Into a large bowl add flour and butter. With a pastry blender cut in butter until mixture looks like fine meal. Add maple sugar, baking powder, baking soda, nutmeg, cinnamon, walnuts, and salt; mix until combined. Make a well in the center of dry ingredients and pour in the milk and maple flavoring.

Mix until just combined and moist. Over-mixing will make the scones tough. Turn the dough out onto a lightly floured surface and knead (being careful not to over-knead) just until it forms a ball. Transfer to a parchment-lined baking sheet and pat or roll into a 1" thick, 8" round. Cut into 8 wedges and separate. Brush with egg white.

Bake at 375°F for 25 minutes. Remove from oven, let rest 3 minutes, and transfer scones to a cooling rack. In a small bowl, combine confectioners' sugar with enough maple syrup to make a glaze. Drizzle over scones and serve.

Maple Cream Cheese Spread with crackers and fruit

Spreads, Dips, and Toppings

Maple Cream Cheese Spread

YIELD: 6 servings, PREP: 10 min

1 cup granulated maple sugar
1 package cream cheese (8 oz.)

Soften cream cheese. With electric mixer, blend cream cheese and maple sugar. Let set 10 minutes and then mix again. This dissolves the maple sugar. A great spread for bagels, fruit, or crackers.

Maple Nut Cream Cheese

YIELD: 1¼ cups, PREP: 10 min

1 tub spreadable cream cheese
   (8 oz)
3 Tbsp. maple syrup
¼ cup raisins
¼ cup pecans, chopped

In a medium bowl, mix cream cheese and maple syrup until well blended. Stir in raisins and pecans. This makes a great spread for sweet breads and bagels.

Though this recipe may seem very similar to the Maple Cream Cheese Spread (above), this one has fruit and nuts and uses maple syrup, which is more readily available than granulated maple sugar.

Maple Cream with Vermont Maple Syrup Grading Kit (page ix)

Maple Cream

YIELD: 3 cups, PREP: 5 min, COOK: 45 min

4 cups maple syrup

Add 4 cups of syrup into a stainless steel pan. Attach candy thermometer and cook syrup over medium heat to 232°F. Remove from heat, remove thermometer, and put in a very cold place to cool.

When your thumb leaves an imprint in the syrup, it is ready to stir. It will be very hard to stir at first – then it will get easier and will lighten in color. When it starts to lose its shine and thickens again, it is ready to put into containers. Stir time is approximately 15 minutes.

Tastes great on toast, English muffins, or even Raised Doughnuts (page 25).

Maple Butter

YIELD: 3 cups, PREP: 8 min plus cooling, COOK: 50 min (approx.)

3 cups maple syrup
1 cup butter (no substitutes)

In large saucepan, cook maple syrup to 235°F on a candy thermometer. Remove from heat and add butter; do not mix. Cool mixture to 120°F and remove thermometer. Beat with mixer until creamy and thick.

This recipe came from our neighbor and fellow sugar maker.

Maple Jelly

YIELD: 1½ cups, PREP: 30 min, COOK: 15 min

1⅓ cup Grade A Dark Amber
   maple syrup
⅓ cup water
1 tsp. unflavored gelatin

In a small bowl, combine gelatin with water and let set for 30 minutes. In a small saucepan, add the maple syrup and gelatin mixture. Heat over low heat, stirring constantly until mixture comes to a hard boil. Remove from heat, put into jelly jars, and refrigerate overnight.

Maple Nut Granola on yogurt

Maple Nut Granola

YIELD: 14 cups, PREP: 25 min, BAKE: 1 hour (approx.)

7 cups rolled oats
½ cup wheat germ
1 cup safflower oil
1 tsp. vanilla
1 cup maple syrup
½ cup shredded coconut
¼ cup golden raisins
¼ cup dates, chopped
¼ cup dried apricots, chopped
¾ cup pecans, coarsely chopped
½ cup sunflower seeds

Heat oven to 350°F. In a large bowl, combine rolled oats and wheat germ. In a small bowl, mix together the oil, vanilla, and maple syrup. Pour this mixture over the dry mixture and stir until well coated, adding more syrup if necessary. Place on a large rimmed baking pan.

Bake 10 minutes then mix with spatula. Repeat every 10 minutes until of desired dryness. Cool and add remaining ingredients. Store in airtight containers. Great served over yogurt and pudding.

Maple Barbecue Sauce

YIELD: 1 cup, PREP: 10 min

¾ cup dark maple syrup
4 tsp. ketchup
1 tsp. Worcestershire sauce
½ tsp. dry mustard
1 tsp. salt
¼ tsp. pepper
1 Tbsp. vinegar
1 small onion, finely chopped

Whisk all ingredients together in a small bowl. Refrigerate until ready to use.

Great on chicken, pork, and baby back ribs.

Maple Salsa

YIELD: 6 servings, PREP: 40 min

6 large red tomatoes
1 large onion, chopped
2 colored peppers, chopped
1 jalapeño pepper, finely chopped
1 Tbsp. garlic, minced
1 bunch scallions, sliced
1 Tbsp. chives, minced
2 Tbsp. cilantro, minced
2 Tbsp. parsley, minced
2 Tbsp. lemon juice
1 Tbsp. lime juice
½ cup maple syrup
2 Tbsp. soy sauce
½ tsp. cayenne pepper
1 tsp. cumin
½ tsp. salt
½ tsp. pepper

Scoop out seeds and pulp from tomatoes and cut into ½-inch pieces. Combine remaining ingredients and mix well.

Refrigerate overnight to let flavors mingle. Stir occasionally.

Serve with corn chips.

Baked Maple Brie and Scallops Wrapped in Bacon with Maple Sausage-Stuffed Mushrooms (page 18)

Appetizers

Baked Maple Brie

YIELD: 8 servings, PREP: 15 min, BAKE: 15 min

1 wheel of Brie with rind (8 oz.)
¼ cup maple syrup
¼ cup coffee liqueur
½ cup pecans, chopped
1 box assorted crackers

Carefully remove the top rind from the Brie. Place Brie on an ovenproof dish and bake at 350°F for 15 minutes.

While Brie is in the oven, make the sauce by combining in a small heavy-duty saucepan the syrup and coffee liqueur. Cook on low heat about 10 minutes or until it just starts to thicken. Add pecans, mixing to coat. Remove from heat.

Remove Brie from oven and pour syrup mixture over the top. Serve with fancy assorted crackers.

Scallops Wrapped in Bacon

YIELD: 4 servings, PREP: 10 min, BAKE: 15 min, BROIL: 10 min

16 large scallops
8 strips of bacon
¾ cup maple syrup

Microwave bacon on a paper towel-lined plate 3 minutes. Cut strips in half and wrap around scallops, securing with a toothpick.

Place in a medium-size baking dish and pour syrup over the scallops. Cover and bake at 375°F for 15 minutes. Remove from oven and baste well.

Return to oven and broil for an additional 10 minutes or until bacon begins to crisp.

Maple Sausage-Stuffed Mushrooms

YIELD: 4 doz, PREP: 40 min, BAKE: 25 min

2 lbs. white button mushrooms
1 lb. pkg. ground sausage
3 Tbsp. dark maple syrup
8 oz. cream cheese, softened
¼ cup Parmesan cheese

Prepare mushrooms by cleaning and removing stem (save for later). Place mushrooms on a rimmed baking sheet. Finely chop mushroom stems to equal ¾ cup. In a large bowl, mix sausage, maple syrup, and chopped mushroom stems until well combined.

Cook sausage mixture in a medium skillet until sausage is no longer pink, about 8 minutes. Drain off fat. Place sausage mixture in a large bowl and cool. Add cream cheese and blend well.

Stuff mushrooms and sprinkle with Parmesan cheese. Bake immediately or cover and refrigerate until ready to use. Bake at 350°F for 25 minutes.

Maple-Glazed Wieners

YIELD: 8 servings, PREP: 5 min, COOK: 15 min

1 lb. cocktail wieners
1 Tbsp. butter
1 Tbsp. soy sauce
¼ cup maple syrup

Combine butter, soy sauce, and maple syrup in a skillet and bring to a simmer. Score wieners and add to sauce. Stir until meat is coated and thick. Serve warm.

Mix it up: Substitute meatballs for the wieners.

Maple Caramelized Onion Bruschetta

YIELD: 24 servings, PREP: 30 min, COOK: 15 min

¼ cup butter
2 large onions, thinly sliced
¼ cup maple syrup
4 Tbsp. rice vinegar
1 lb. French baguette
1 tub of soft cream cheese
with herbs (8 oz.)
1 Tbsp. chives, minced

In a large skillet, heat butter. When hot, add onions and cook 5 minutes or until onions are soft. Add maple syrup and vinegar. Cook, stirring frequently, until onions are caramelized, about 10 minutes. Cool mixture, about 10 minutes.

While cooking onions, toast the bread by slicing ¼ inch thick and placing on a cookie sheet. Broil 3 inches from heat, 2 minutes. Turn over bread slices and broil an additional 2 minutes. Remove from oven, spread cream cheese on toast, and top with 1 tsp. of caramelized onions. Garnish with fresh chives.

Maple Date Nut Bread with Maple Cream Cheese Spread (page 11)

Bread, Doughnuts, etc.

Maple Date Nut Bread

YIELD: 1 loaf, PREP: 20 min, BAKE: 1 hour

1 cup dates, chopped
1 cup boiling water
1 egg, beaten
½ cup maple syrup
½ tsp. natural maple flavoring*
1 Tbsp. butter, melted
1 tsp. salt
¾ tsp. baking soda
1 tsp. baking powder
2 cups flour
½ cup walnuts, chopped

*Refer to page ix.

Combine dates and boiling water in large mixing bowl and let set 5 minutes. Add remaining ingredients and beat well. Pour into greased loaf pan and bake for 1 hour at 350°F. Remove from oven to cooling rack.

Great with Maple Cream Cheese Spread (page 11).

Maple Oatmeal Bread

YIELD: 2 loaves, PREP: 20 min plus 3-hour rise, BAKE: 35 min

2 cups rolled oats
1 Tbsp. butter
2 cups boiling water
½ cup maple syrup
½ tsp. natural maple flavoring*
1 tsp. salt
1 pkg. yeast
5 cups flour
Melted butter for brushing on baked bread

*Refer to page ix.

Place oats, butter, and boiling water in bowl and microwave on high for 3 minutes. Set aside and cool to lukewarm. Add maple syrup and maple flavoring to oat mixture. Combine flour, yeast, and salt. Add to oat mixture and mix well.

Turn out onto floured board and knead until smooth and elastic about 8 to 10 minutes. Place in a large buttered bowl, cover and let rise until double in bulk. Punch down and turn out onto floured board, knead for 2 minutes and divide into two loaves. Let rise until double or 1 inch higher than the edge of pan. Bake at 350°F for 35 to 40 minutes. Remove from pan and brush top with melted butter.

Anadama Bread Rolls

YIELD: 2 loaves (2 doz rolls), PREP: 20 min plus 2½ hour rise, BAKE: 45 min

½ cup cornmeal
2 cups boiling water
2 Tbsp. shortening
½ cup dark maple syrup
2 tsp. salt
1 pkg. yeast
½ cup warm water
5-6 cups flour
Melted butter for brushing on baked bread

In a large bowl, add boiling water and slowly stir in cornmeal until thoroughly mixed. Add shortening, syrup, and salt.

When mixture is lukewarm, add yeast dissolved in ½ cup of warm water. Stir in 5 to 6 cups flour, enough to make a stiff dough. Knead for 10 minutes.

Place in well-greased bowl, cover with greased plastic wrap, and let rise until double, about 2 hours.

Punch down and knead again. Shape into two loaves or two dozen rolls and place in greased pans. Let rise until 1 inch higher than edge of pan, about 30 minutes. Bake at 375°F for 45 minutes. Turn out onto cooling rack and brush with melted butter.

Maple Shredded Wheat Bread Rolls

YIELD: 2 loaves (2 doz rolls), PREP: 20 min plus 3 hour rise, BAKE: 30-40 min

2 large shredded wheat biscuits
2 cups boiling water
3 Tbsp. butter
½ cup maple syrup
⅓ cup sugar
1 Tbsp. salt
1 pkg. yeast
¼ cup lukewarm water
6½ cups flour
Melted butter for brushing on baked bread

Place shredded wheat biscuits into a large bowl; cover with boiling water. To this mixture add the butter, maple syrup, sugar, and salt. Stir to melt the butter. Cool to 105°F on an instant-read thermometer.

Dissolve yeast in warm water (95-104°F) and stir into shredded wheat mixture. Stir in flour to make a stiff dough. Knead until smooth. Place dough in greased bowl and cover with plastic wrap. Place bowl in warm place to let rise until double in size.

Punch down, knead again and shape into two loaves or two dozen rolls. Place in greased pans, cover, let rise again until 1 inch higher than edge of pan. Bake at 375°F for 40 minutes. Remove from pan and brush with melted butter.

Sweet Maple Doughnuts

YIELD: 5 doz, PREP: 20 min, COOK: 3 min

5½ cups flour
4 tsp. baking powder
1 tsp. baking soda
¾ tsp. salt
1 tsp. ginger
1 tsp. nutmeg
¾ cup maple sugar
Shortening the size of an egg
¾ cup maple syrup
3 eggs
1½ cups sour milk
1 tsp. vanilla

Sift together flour, baking powder, baking soda, salt, ginger, and nutmeg; set aside. In large mixing bowl beat sugar, shortening, syrup, eggs, milk, and vanilla. Add flour mixture, beating well. Stir to a soft dough. Roll out dough to ½ inch thick and cut with a doughnut cutter. Heat oil to 370°F. Drop doughnuts into hot oil and fry until golden brown, turning when they rise to the surface.

I have left the ingredient listing exactly the way it has been for generations. Shortening the size of an egg is approximately ⅓ cup. Sour milk can be made by adding a small amount of vinegar to the bottom of a measuring cup before adding milk.

Raised Doughnuts

YIELD: 5 doz, PREP: 25 min plus 3-hour rise, COOK: 3 min

¾ cup shortening
2⅔ cup hot milk
¾ cup sugar
3 tsp. salt
3 eggs, beaten
3 pkg. yeast, dissolved in ¾ cup
   warm water
9-10 cups flour

Put shortening in large bowl and add hot milk, sugar, and salt. Stir until shortening is melted and cool to lukewarm. Add the eggs and the yeast dissolved in water. Mix in flour, two cups at a time, mixing well after each addition.

Turn out onto floured surface and knead 10 minutes. Place in an extra-large greased bowl and let rise until double. Punch down and turn out on floured surface. Roll to ½ inch thick and cut with a doughnut cutter. Let rise 1 hour. Fry in 370°F oil until golden, turning once. Remove from oil; cool. As an option, spread with *Maple Glaze (page 58)*.

My mother would spend days in the winter making and freezing raised doughnuts in preparation for the spring sugar season. These are traditionally served with Sugar on Snow (page 3).

Maple Bran Muffins

YIELD: 12 muffins, PREP: 15 min, BAKE: 25 min

1 cup flour
1 cup all-bran cereal
½ tsp. salt
1 tsp. baking powder
½ tsp. baking soda
½ cup raisins
½ cup walnuts, chopped
1 cup sour cream
⅔ cup maple syrup
3 eggs, beaten

In a large bowl, combine flour, all-bran, salt, baking powder, baking soda, raisins, and walnuts. In a medium bowl combine the sour cream, maple syrup, and eggs. Add egg mixture to the dry ingredients and mix just until combined and moistened. Fill greased muffin tins ⅔ full and bake at 350°F for 25 minutes.

Maple Date Nut Muffins

YIELD: 12 muffins, PREP: 20 min, BAKE: 25 min

1 large egg
½ cup maple syrup
½ cup milk
¼ cup butter, melted
¼ cup sugar
2 cups flour
3 tsp. baking powder
½ tsp. salt
½ cup dates, chopped
½ cup walnuts, chopped

In a large bowl, beat egg, syrup, milk, and melted butter. Add dry ingredients and mix just until moistened. Mix in dates and nuts just until combined. Do not over-mix. Fill greased muffin tins ⅔ full and bake at 350°F for 25 minutes.

Maple Corn Muffins

YIELD: 12 muffins, PREP: 15 min, BAKE: 25 min

1 cup flour
2 tsp. baking powder
½ tsp. baking soda
⅔ cup cornmeal
½ tsp. salt
2 eggs, beaten
8 oz. plain or vanilla yogurt
½ cup dark maple syrup
¼ cup vegetable oil

In a large bowl combine dry ingredients. Add eggs, yogurt, maple syrup, and oil. Mix just until moistened. Fill greased muffin tins ⅔ full and bake at 350°F for 25 minutes.

Maple Sugar Rugelach

YIELD: 16 rolls, PREP: 15 min, BAKE: 20 min

2 cans refrigerated crescent rolls
½ cup granulated maple sugar
1 cup walnuts, finely chopped
1 egg, beaten

Combine in a small bowl maple sugar and walnuts. Unroll crescent rolls and separate. Brush dough with egg. Sprinkle sugar mixture on rolls. Starting at a corner, roll up and place on cookie sheet. Bake at 350°F for 20 minutes.

Maple Monkey Bread

YIELD: 10 servings, PREP: 20 min, BAKE: 40 min

2 cans refrigerated buttermilk biscuits
½ cup white sugar
1 tsp. cinnamon
¾ cup pecans, chopped
¾ cup butter, melted
1 cup granulated maple sugar

Open cans of biscuits and separate, cut biscuits into quarters and place into a large mixing bowl. Combine white sugar and cinnamon in a small bowl, sprinkle over biscuits, and toss to coat.

Place biscuit pieces into a greased fluted or tube pan, adding pecans among the biscuits. Meanwhile, melt butter and maple sugar in a small pan. Pour over biscuits.

Bake at 350°F for 30 minutes or until pick inserted into bread comes out clean. Remove from oven and let rest 10 minutes. Turn upside down onto a serving plate.

Maple Pecan Sticky Buns

YIELD: 12 buns, PREP: 20 min plus 2-hour rise, BAKE: 30 min

3 cups flour
¼ cup sugar
1 pkg. rapid-rise yeast
1 tsp. salt
1 cup warm water
   (120-130°F)
6 Tbsp. butter, divided
1 cup chopped pecans
½ cup maple syrup
1 egg, room temp., beaten
½ cup granulated maple sugar
1 tsp. cinnamon

In a large bowl, combine 2 cups flour, sugar, yeast, and salt. Stir in water, 2 tablespoons of butter, and egg. Beat until smooth, gradually adding remaining flour until soft dough forms. Cover with greased plastic wrap and let rise until double.

Grease a 13" x 9" baking pan. Spread pecans and syrup evenly over bottom of pan. On lightly floured surface, roll dough into a 15" x 12" rectangle. Spread with remaining butter. Mix maple sugar with cinnamon; sprinkle over the dough.

Starting with the 12" side, roll up tightly. Cut into 12 slices and place in prepared pan. Cover with greased plastic wrap and let rise until double, about 30-45 minutes.

Preheat oven to 375°F, uncover buns and bake until golden, 25-30 minutes. Cool for 1 minute. Loosen edges and invert onto a serving plate.

L to R: Sweet & Sour Maple Dressing, Maple Vinaigrette, French Maple Dressing

Salads and Dressings

Sweet & Sour Maple Dressing

YIELD: 2½ cups, PREP: 10 min

1 cup maple syrup
½ cup canola oil
½ cup ketchup
½ cup white vinegar
1 tsp. minced garlic
2 tsp. horseradish

In a medium bowl, whisk together syrup, oil, ketchup, vinegar, garlic, and horseradish. Pour into a dressing bottle and refrigerate overnight to blend the flavors. Shake well before serving.

Maple Vinaigrette

YIELD: 1 cup, PREP: 10 min

1 tsp. dry mustard
½ tsp. dried basil
¼ cup white wine vinegar
½ cup maple syrup
1 Tbsp. lemon juice
1 clove minced garlic
1 tsp. salt
¼ tsp. black pepper

In a pint mason jar, mix all ingredients and shake vigorously. Pour into vinaigrette bottle and serve over your favorite mixed greens salad. The dressing will last for several weeks refrigerated.

French Maple Dressing

YIELD: 1½ cups, PREP: 8 min plus 2-hour refrigeration

⅓ cup maple syrup
½ cup canola oil
½ cup ketchup
⅓ cup white vinegar
2 cloves garlic, crushed
2 tsp. Worcestershire sauce
1 tsp. paprika
½ tsp. each salt and pepper

Whisk all ingredients together in a small bowl. Pour into a dressing bottle and refrigerate 2 hours to blend the flavors. Shake well before serving.

Cabbage Fruit Salad

YIELD: 6 servings, PREP: 15 min

1 small head of cabbage
1 large Red Delicious apple
½ cup raisins
½ cup walnuts, chopped
½ cup mayonnaise
2 Tbsp. dark maple syrup

On a large cutting board, chop cabbage and add to a large bowl. Core the apple, cut into chunks, and add to the bowl along with the raisins and walnuts.

Make the dressing by whisking together the mayonnaise and syrup and pour over the cabbage mixture. Mix well and serve.

Spinach Salad w/ Hot Maple Bacon Dressing

YIELD: 4 servings, PREP: 25 min, COOK: 10 min

1 roasted red pepper
1 lb. baby spinach
1 red onion, sliced
½ lb. smoked bacon
6 Tbsp. maple syrup
6 Tbsp. rice vinegar
½ tsp. salt
½ tsp. pepper
½ cup sliced almonds

Prepare salad by first roasting red pepper in the oven, on the stove or on the grill, until charred. Remove from heat, place in a bowl and cover until cool. Remove skin from roasted pepper and slice. In a large bowl add spinach, red onion, and roasted pepper.

Cook bacon in cast iron pan over medium heat until crisp. Drain on paper towels. Break into medium pieces; save for garnish. Stir maple syrup into pan used for bacon. Add vinegar and salt and pepper to taste.

Serve dressing hot over spinach salad. Garnish with bacon crumbles and sliced almonds.

Maple Walnut Dressing

YIELD: 1½ cups, PREP: 10 min

½ cup cider vinegar
½ cup maple syrup
2 Tbsp. whole grain Dijon
   mustard
¼ cup walnut oil
½ tsp. salt
½ tsp. pepper

Whisk all ingredients together in a small bowl. Pour into a vinaigrette bottle and refrigerate. Shake well before using.

Vegetables and Sides

Roasted Veggies with Maple Drizzle

YIELD: 4 servings, PREP: 15 min plus 8 min parboil, BAKE: 30 min

½ lb. Brussels sprouts
½ lb. carrots, sliced
½ lb. cauliflower florets
½ lb. baby potatoes, halved
2 large onions, quartered
3 Tbsp. olive oil
3 Tbsp. fancy maple syrup

Prepare all vegetables and parboil 8 minutes. Drain and place in a large mixing bowl, drizzle with olive oil, and salt to taste. Pour onto a large rimmed baking pan.

Bake at 375°F for 30 minutes, turning halfway through. Remove from oven. Place onto a serving dish and drizzle with maple syrup.

Any combination of vegetables can be used that equals 2 pounds.

Maple-Glazed Carrots

YIELD: 6 servings, PREP: 20 min, COOK: 20 min

1 lb. or 3 cups carrots
4 Tbsp. butter
⅓ cup maple syrup
⅓ cup golden raisins, optional

Peel and slice carrots into ½-inch medallions. Place in medium saucepan of boiling water, and cook until tender. Drain and add butter, maple syrup, and raisins. Simmer in syrup, stirring occasionally until carrots and raisins are glazed.

Maple Sugar-Dusted Sweet Potato Fries

YIELD: 4 servings, PREP: 15 min, COOK: 20 min

2 large sweet potatoes, unpeeled
¼ cup maple sugar
¼ tsp. cinnamon
1 tsp. Kosher salt
Oil for frying

Half fill a heavy-duty pot with oil or use a deep fryer. Heat oil to 350°F. Combine maple sugar and cinnamon in a small bowl and set aside. Scrub sweet potatoes clean. Cut into wedges. Fry half the wedges in hot oil, turning to brown all sides, about 10 minutes.

Remove to a paper towel-lined pan and sprinkle with half of the sugar mixture and ½ tsp. salt. Cover to keep warm while frying the second batch of wedges. Remove second batch from fryer, drain, and sprinkle with remaining maple sugar and salt. Serve immediately.

Maple Acorn Squash

YIELD: 6 servings, PREP: 15 min, BAKE: 45 min

3 acorn squash
18 Tbsp. maple syrup
6 tsp. butter

Clean squash by cutting in half and removing pulp and seeds. Place halved squash in lightly greased casserole dish. Score inside of squash. To each half, add 3 Tbsp. of maple syrup and 1 tsp. of butter. Bake at 375°F for 45 minutes or until done.

Maple Cream Cheese Salad

YIELD: 8 servings, PREP: 20 min

1 package cream cheese,
   softened (8 oz.)
1 cup maple syrup
1 cup dates, chopped
1 cup walnuts, chopped
1 can crushed pineapple, drained
1 container of Cool Whip (8 oz.)

In a large bowl, beat the cream cheese and maple syrup. Add the pineapple, dates and walnuts, mix well. This will look curdled but will blend in when you add the Cool Whip. Fold in Cool Whip. Chill.

Mom entered this recipe at the Vermont Farm Show and won a blue ribbon. This recipe is a family favorite at our Christmas dinner.

Sweet Potato Bake

YIELD: 8 servings, PREP: 20 min, BAKE: 1 hour

4 cups mashed sweet potato
1 Tbsp. butter
3 Tbsp. maple syrup
1 egg, beaten
½ cup milk
½ cup pecans or walnuts, chopped
½ cup granulated maple sugar
1 Tbsp. flour
1 Tbsp. melted butter

Spray a 1½- to 2-quart casserole dish with cooking spray. In a large bowl, with hand-held electric mixer, blend sweet potato, butter, and syrup. Beat in egg and milk. Pour into prepared casserole dish.

Combine nuts, maple sugar and flour in bowl; stir in melted butter. Sprinkle over sweet potatoes. Bake at 350°F for 1 hour.

Refrigerator Pickles

YIELD: 3 pints, PREP: 30 min

3 cups sugar
1 cup dark maple syrup
4 cups vinegar
½ cup canning salt
1 Tbsp. celery salt
1 Tbsp. mustard seed
1 Tbsp. turmeric
3 onions, sliced
1 lb. cucumbers, sliced thin

Combine sugar, syrup, vinegar, salt, and spices to make a cold syrup. Do not heat. Place cucumbers in glass jars and cover with cold syrup. Refrigerate for 5 days before using. Keeps for 6 months in the refrigerator.

Bourbon Maple Flank Steak with garlic mashed potatoes

Entrées

Bourbon Maple Flank Steak

YIELD: 4 servings, PREP: 10 min plus marinating time, GRILL: 10 min

¼ cup dark maple syrup
¼ cup minced green onions
¼ cup soy sauce
¼ cup Dijon mustard
¼ cup Kentucky Bourbon
½ tsp. fresh ground black pepper
¼ tsp. Worcestershire sauce
2 lbs. flank steak
1 Tbsp. cornstarch
Fresh chives, minced

Make a marinade by combining in a gallon-size zip-close plastic bag the sugar, onions, soy sauce, mustard, Bourbon, pepper, and Worcestershire sauce. Add steak; seal and marinate in refrigerator 8 hours, turning bag occasionally.

Remove steak from bag, reserve marinade for later. Preheat grill, spray with cooking spray, place steak on grill, and grill 5 minutes on each side. Let stand 10 minutes. Cut diagonally across grain into thin slices.

Optionally, use the leftover marinade to make a brown gravy. In small pan combine reserved marinade with 1 Tbsp. of cornstarch and bring to a boil, stirring constantly. Boil 1 minute. Serve gravy over steak. Garnish with fresh chives.

Goes great with garlic mashed potatoes!

Maple Baked Chicken

YIELD: 4 servings, PREP: 20 min, BAKE: 40 min

2 lbs. chicken
1½ cups maple syrup to coat
2 cups crunchy topping, such as crushed corn flakes, potato chips, or panko flakes

Remove skin from chicken. Dip in maple syrup, coating well. Roll in topping. Place in baking pan and bake at 375°F for 40 minutes or until done.

This is an excellent recipe given to me by my friend Lenny and is super easy to make.

Sweet & Sour Chicken

YIELD: 6 servings, PREP: 15 min, COOK: 15 min

1 cup pineapple chunks,
  drained (save juice)
3 cups uncooked chicken, cubed
1 Tbsp. cooking oil
⅓ cup maple syrup
¼ cup white vinegar
1 Tbsp. soy sauce
½ cup pineapple juice
2 Tbsp. cornstarch
½ tsp. salt
1 medium onion, chopped
½ cup celery, chopped
½ cup green pepper, chopped
¼ cup maraschino cherries,
  cut in half
2½ cups cooked rice

Drain pineapple; save ½ cup of the juice. Make sweet-and-sour sauce by whisking in a small bowl the maple syrup, vinegar, soy sauce, pineapple juice, corn starch, and salt; set aside.

Heat a large skillet or wok until very hot; add cooking oil to coat. Spread out chicken in pan and fry without turning until browned on the bottom, about 2 minutes. Turn over chicken and continue frying an additional 2 minutes or until cooked through. Remove chicken and set aside.

To the skillet or wok add a drizzle of cooking oil, heat pan until hot and immediately add the onion, celery, and green pepper. Fry 1-2 minutes, turning as needed.

Reduce heat to medium. Add the cooked chicken to the skillet or wok. Whisk the sweet-and-sour sauce and pour over the chicken and vegetables, stirring and cooking until thick. Add pineapple chunks and cherries. Simmer 5 minutes. Serve over cooked rice.

Pictured with sweet potatoes and Cabbage Fruit Salad (page 32)

Maple Mustard Pork Chops

YIELD: 4 servings, PREP: 30 min, COOK: 10 min

4 bone-in pork chops
¼ tsp. salt
¼ tsp. fresh ground pepper
1 Tbsp. butter
2 Tbsp. onions, finely chopped
¼ cup chicken broth
2 Tbsp. Dijon mustard
2 Tbsp. maple syrup
2 Tbsp. fresh parsley, chopped

Salt and pepper both sides of pork chops. Heat a large cast iron pan over medium heat. Spray with cooking spray. Add pork chops to pan and cook 3 minutes on each side. Remove from pan and keep warm.

Return skillet to heat; add butter and onion. Sauté until translucent. In a small bowl, whisk together broth, mustard, and syrup. Add to pan, bring to a boil, and cook 1 minute or until slightly thick. Serve pork chops with maple mustard sauce.

Slow-Cooked Maple Ham

YIELD: 10 servings, PREP: 10 min, COOK: 6-8 hours

6 lb. ham, boneless
1 cup maple sugar
½ cup maple syrup
2 cups pineapple juice

Into a large slow cooker add the ham. Rub maple sugar on all sides. Add the maple syrup and pineapple juice. Cover and cook on low for 6-8 hours. Baste ham with juices from the bottom of the slow cooker an hour or so before serving. When cooking is done, remove carefully and let it rest on a cutting board for 15-20 minutes before carving.

Pan-Seared Scallops

YIELD: 2 servings, PREP: 10 min plus 1 hour marinating time, COOK: 6 min

12 sea scallops
¼ cup maple syrup
1 Tbsp. Dijon mustard
1 Tbsp. horseradish
1 Tbsp. butter

Make a marinade of the maple syrup, mustard, and horseradish by combining in a bowl and mixing well. Rinse scallops and remove tough muscle. Place in a zip-close plastic bag, add marinade, and refrigerate for 1 hour, turning once after 30 minutes.

Drain scallops and lightly pat dry. Heat a large skillet with butter. Add scallops and cook until done, about 3 minutes per side. Season with salt and pepper and serve.

Maple Nut Salmon

YIELD: 4 servings, PREP: 8 min, BAKE: 15 min

4 (6 oz.) fillets
4 Tbsp. maple syrup
1 Tbsp. oil
⅓ cup walnuts, chopped
Salt and pepper to taste

Preheat oven to 375°F. Place salmon on non-stick foil-lined baking pan. Sprinkle with salt and pepper. Drizzle with maple syrup. Bake for 15 minutes or until fish flakes easily. Toast walnuts in skillet with 1 Tbsp. oil for 1 minute. Spoon over salmon and serve.

Mom's Baked Beans

YIELD: 10 servings, PREP: 1 hour plus overnight soaking, BAKE: 1 hour

2 lbs. soldier beans
½ tsp. baking soda
2 cups dark maple syrup
¼ cup molasses
2 tsp. dry mustard
1½ tsp. salt
½ tsp. pepper
2 small onions
1 lb. smoked bacon

Soak beans overnight in large kettle. In the morning rinse beans and return to kettle, add water to cover, and boil until skins crack, about 50 minutes. Add ½ tsp. baking soda and boil 10 minutes.

Drain and rinse beans and place into large casserole dish. Mix in maple syrup, molasses, mustard, salt, and pepper. Push whole small onions into the beans and top with bacon. Add water to cover beans. Bake at 350°F for 1 hour. Add more water as needed.

One of the recipes that I presented on the TV show "Across the Fence."

Desserts

Vermont Pumpkin Pie

YIELD: 6 servings, PREP: 20 min, BAKE: 1 hour

3 eggs
1 can pumpkin (15 oz.)
¾ cup dark maple syrup
½ tsp. cinnamon
½ tsp. nutmeg
½ tsp. ginger
1 Tbsp. cornstarch
½ tsp. salt
1½ cups evaporated milk
2 Tbsp. butter, melted
1 unbaked 9" pie shell

Beat eggs in a large mixing bowl. Add pumpkin, maple syrup, spices, cornstarch, and salt; mix well. With electric mixer on low speed, mix in evaporated milk and butter. Pour into unbaked pie shell. Bake at 350°F for 1 hour or until just firm in the middle. Cool.

Maple Pecan Pie

YIELD: 6 servings, PREP: 15 min, BAKE: 40-50 min

3 eggs
¾ cup sugar
1 cup maple syrup
1 Tbsp. flour
⅓ tsp. salt
¼ cup butter, melted
1 tsp. vanilla
1 cup pecans
1 unbaked 9" pie shell

Beat eggs, sugar, and syrup. Add flour, salt ,melted butter, and vanilla; mix well. Stir in pecans. Pour into pie shell and bake at 350°F for 40 to 50 minutes or until knife inserted in center comes out clean.

Maple Buttermilk Pie

YIELD: 6 servings, PREP: 20 min, BAKE: 55 min

1 baked 9" pie shell
6 large eggs
2 cups buttermilk, well shaken
⅔ cup dark maple syrup
¼ cup flour
1 tsp. vanilla
¼ tsp. salt

In a large mixing bowl, beat eggs. Add buttermilk, syrup, flour, vanilla and salt. Pour into pie shell. Place pie into a shallow baking pan half-filled with water. Place pan in middle of oven. Bake at 350°F until set in center, about 55 minutes. Transfer pie to cooling rack. Serve warm or cooled with whipped cream.

Vermont Maple Cream Pie

YIELD: 6 servings, PREP: 10 min, COOK: 30 min

1 baked 9" pie shell
2 cups dark maple syrup
2 eggs, beaten
2 cups milk
⅔ cup flour
2 tsp. vanilla

Pour maple syrup into the top of a double boiler. Place pan over direct heat and heat maple syrup just to a boil. In medium bowl, beat eggs; add milk and flour, beating well. Place pan of syrup over water in the bottom of double boiler. Whisk milk mixture slowly into the hot syrup. Cook slowly until thick. Stir in vanilla and pour into baked pie shell and cool completely. Top with *Maple Whipped Cream* (page 61) and serve.

Apple Crisp

YIELD: 8 servings, PREP: 30 min, BAKE: 40 min

4 cups apples, sliced
¾ cup granulated maple sugar
1 Tbsp. flour
¼ tsp. salt
½ tsp. cinnamon

Topping:
½ cup flour
⅛ tsp. baking soda
⅛ tsp. baking powder
¼ cup butter
½ cup oatmeal
½ cup granulated maple sugar

In small bowl combine sugar, flour, salt, and cinnamon. Placed sliced apples into a medium buttered casserole dish. Pour sugar mixture over apples and mix.

In a medium bowl, mix flour, baking soda, and baking powder. Add butter and cut in with a pastry blender until mealy. Mix in maple sugar and oatmeal and spread over apples. Bake at 350°F for 40 minutes.

Vermont Cheesecake

YIELD: 12 servings, PREP: 20 min, BAKE: 1 hour 10 min

4 cups graham cracker crumbs
½ cup sugar
½ cup butter, melted
24 oz. cream cheese, softened
5 eggs
1 cup maple sugar
½ tsp. natural maple flavoring*
16 oz. sour cream
½ cup maple sugar

*Refer to page ix.

Combine graham cracker crumbs, sugar, and melted butter in a large bowl. Press crumb mixture into the bottom and up the sides of a 10-inch springform pan. Set aside. In a large bowl, mix cream cheese and eggs, one at a time, until smooth and creamy. Add maple sugar and maple flavoring. Pour into prepared springform pan.

Bake at 325°F for 1 hour or until set in the middle. Remove from oven and cool 10 minutes. Increase oven temperature to 375°F. Meanwhile, in a small bowl, mix sour cream and maple sugar. Pour over cheesecake, return to oven, and bake an additional 10 minutes. Cool and refrigerate. Drizzle with syrup before serving.

Vermont Pudding Cake

YIELD: 9 servings, PREP: 20 min, BAKE: 40 min

1½ cups flour
¾ cup granulated maple sugar
2 tsp. baking powder
½ tsp. salt
¾ cup milk
1½ cups dark maple syrup
¾ cup water
3 Tbsp. butter

Grease 9" x 9" baking dish. Combine flour, maple sugar, baking powder, salt, and milk. Pour batter into prepared baking dish. In medium saucepan combine syrup, water, and butter. Heat until butter is melted. Pour over batter in baking dish. Bake at 350°F for 40 minutes or until toothpick inserted in cake comes out clean.

Maple Gingerbread

YIELD: 9 servings, PREP: 15 min, BAKE: 30 min

2 eggs
1 cup dark maple syrup
1 cup sour cream
2 cups flour
½ tsp. salt
1 tsp. baking soda
1 tsp. ginger
½ tsp. cinnamon

In a large mixing bowl, beat eggs, syrup, and sour cream. Add flour, salt, baking soda, ginger, and cinnamon; mix well. Pour into greased 9" x 9" baking pan. Bake at 350°F for 30 minutes.

Serve with Maple Whipped Cream (page 61).

Sour Cream Maple Cake

YIELD: 9 servings, PREP: 10 min, BAKE: 30 min

2 eggs
1 cup dark maple sugar
1 cup sour cream
1½ cup flour
1 tsp. baking soda
½ tsp. salt
½ tsp. vanilla

Beat eggs and sugar. Mix in sour cream, flour, baking soda, salt, and vanilla, beating until well combined. Pour into a greased 9" square pan. Bake at 350°F for 30 minutes.

Frost with *Seven-Minute Maple Frosting* (page 55) or serve with *Maple Ice Cream Sauce* (page 73).

Dad's Favorite Maple Cake

YIELD: 16 servings, PREP: 20 min, BAKE: 30 min

2 cups maple sugar
2 eggs
Shortening as big as an egg
1½ cups sour milk
1½ tsp. baking soda
½ tsp. cinnamon
½ tsp. cloves
2½ cups flour
½ tsp. salt

Cream together sugar, shortening, and eggs; beat well. Add baking soda, cinnamon, cloves, and salt. Mix, alternating flour and sour milk, until well blended. Pour into greased 13" x 9" or two greased 9" round pans. Bake at 350°F for 30 minutes or until toothpick inserted in center comes out clean. Top with *Seven-Minute Maple Frosting* (below).

This cake is usually my dad's birthday cake.

Seven-Minute Maple Frosting

YIELD: 4 cups, PREP: 8 min, COOK: 10 min

1 cup granulated maple sugar
3 egg whites
4 Tbsp. water
¼ tsp. cream of tarter

In top of double boiler, combine all ingredients. Cook over boiling water, beating with hand-held electric mixer until stiff peaks form. Remove from heat and continue mixing until cool and of spreading consistency. Yields enough for a 13" x 9" cake or one double layer cake.

Maple Chiffon Cake

YIELD: 15 servings, PREP: 20 min, BAKE: 1 hour

2 cups flour
¾ cup sugar
1 tsp. salt
1 Tbsp. baking powder
1 cup granulated maple sugar
8 egg yolks
8 egg whites
½ cup vegetable oil
¾ cup water
½ tsp. natural maple flavoring*
1 tsp. cream of tarter

*Refer to page ix.

In a medium mixing bowl combine flour, sugar, salt, baking powder, and maple sugar. In a small bowl beat egg yolks with water and maple flavoring. Add to flour mixture and beat well. Set aside.

Into a large mixing bowl add egg whites and cream of tarter. With electric mixer on high speed, beat egg whites until stiff peaks form. Fold cake batter into egg whites, blending well. Pour into a tube pan and bake at 350°F for 1 hour. Remove from oven and invert until cool, approximately 1½ hours.

One of the recipes that I presented on the TV show "Across the Fence."

Maple Apple Cake

YIELD: 12 servings, PREP: 15 min, BAKE: 1 hour

4 eggs
¼ cup maple syrup
1 cup vegetable oil
½ tsp. natural maple flavoring*
2¼ cup flour
1 cup white sugar
1 cup granulated maple sugar
1½ tsp. baking soda
1½ tsp. cinnamon
1 tsp. salt
3 cups apples, chopped
1 cup pecans, chopped

*Refer to page ix.

In a large mixing bowl, beat eggs, syrup, oil, and maple flavoring. In a medium bowl, combine flour, white sugar, maple sugar, baking soda, cinnamon, and salt. Add to the egg mixture and mix until blended. Stir in apples and pecans.

Pour batter into a greased and floured bundt cake pan. Bake in a 350 degree oven for 1 hour or until a cake tester inserted in the center comes out clean.

Remove from oven and let rest 10 minutes before removing from pan. Invert onto a plate and while still warm spread with *Maple Pecan Glaze* (below).

Maple Pecan Glaze

YIELD: 1 cup, PREP: 3 min, COOK: 15-20 min

¾ cup maple syrup
1 cup heavy cream
½ cup pecans, chopped

In saucepan, combine syrup and cream. Bring to a boil. Boil rapidly 15 to 20 minutes or until thickened, stirring occasionally. Add pecans and spread over cheesecake or ice cream.

Maple Pound Cake

YIELD: 12 servings, PREP: 20 min, BAKE: 1 hour 15 min

  1 cup butter, softened
1½ cups granulated sugar
  ½ cup maple sugar
2¼ cups flour
  1 tsp. baking powder
  ½ tsp. salt
  ¼ cup milk
  1 tsp. natural maple flavoring*
  5 eggs
1½ cups walnuts, chopped

*Refer to page ix.

In large mixing bowl, cream butter and sugars until fluffy. In another bowl, combine all dry ingredients. In measuring cup, mix milk and maple flavoring. Beat into butter mixture alternating with the flour mixture. Beat in eggs one at a time. Mix in walnuts, saving ¼ cup for garnish.

Pour into greased 10-inch tube pan or large greased loaf pan. Bake at 350°F in lower third of oven for approximately 1 hour 15 minutes, just until pick inserted in center comes out clean. Cool in pan 15 minutes and then turn out onto cooling rack. When cool, drizzle with *Maple Glaze* (below) and garnish with remaining walnuts.

Maple Glaze

YIELD: 1 cup, PREP: 5 min

1½ cups confectioners' sugar
  ¼ cup maple syrup (approx.)

Blend confectioners' sugar with enough maple syrup to make a glaze consistency.

Maple Pecan Loaf

YIELD: 12 servings, PREP: 22 min, BAKE: 1 hour

2¼ cups flour
¾ cup granulated maple sugar
1 cup light cream
3 Tbsp. vegetable oil
3½ tsp. baking powder
½ tsp. natural maple flavoring*
½ tsp. salt
1 egg
½ cup pecans, chopped

Glaze:
½ cup confectioners' sugar
2 Tbsp. maple syrup
2 Tbsp. pecans, chopped

*Refer to page ix.

Prepare loaf pan by greasing bottom with shortening. In a large bowl, mix flour, maple sugar, cream, oil, baking powder, maple flavoring, salt, and egg; beat 30 seconds. Stir in chopped pecans. Pour into prepared pan.

Bake 1 hour or until toothpick inserted in center comes out clean. Cool 10 minutes. Loosen sides of loaf from pan; remove from pan to wire rack. Cool completely.

Make glaze by combining ½ cup confectioners' sugar and 2 tablespoons of maple syrup. Mix until thin enough to drizzle over loaf. Sprinkle with 2 tablespoons of chopped pecans.

Maple Pecan Squares

YIELD: 9 servings, PREP: 30 min, BAKE: 40 min total

Crust:
1 cup flour
¼ cup brown sugar, packed
½ cup butter, softened

Topping:
⅔ cup brown sugar, packed
1 cup maple syrup
2 eggs, beaten
¼ cup butter, softened
¼ tsp. salt
½ tsp. vanilla
2 Tbsp. flour
⅔ cup pecan halves

In a large bowl, mix flour, brown sugar, and butter. Press into 9" x 9" pan. Bake 10 minutes at 350°F.

Combine sugar and syrup in a small saucepan and simmer 5 minutes. Cool. Mix eggs into syrup mixture. Stir in butter, salt, vanilla, flour, and pecan halves. Spread over crust. Bake at 450°F for 10 minutes. Reduce to 350°F and bake an additional 20 minutes.

Maple Bread Pudding

YIELD: 8 servings, PREP: 15 min, BAKE: 1 hour

7 slices day-old bread
3 eggs, beaten
1 cup maple syrup
½ tsp. salt
¼ tsp. nutmeg
3 cups milk, scalded
½ cup raisins (optional)

Grease a medium-size casserole dish. Cut bread into 1-inch pieces and place in casserole dish. In a large mixing bowl, beat the eggs, maple syrup, salt, and nutmeg. While beating, slowly add scalded milk; mix in raisins and pour over bread in casserole dish. Let sit until bread absorbs milk. Sprinkle with additional nutmeg. Place casserole in a baking pan half-filled with water. Bake at 350°F for 1 hour or until knife inserted in center comes out clean. Serve with *Maple Rum Sauce* (below).

Maple Rum Sauce

YIELD: 1½ cups, PREP: 8 min, COOK: 10 min

¾ cup heavy cream
¼ cup dark maple syrup
¼ cup brown sugar
¼ cup rum
2 tsp. cornstarch
2 tsp. rum

In a small heavy-bottomed saucepan, combine cream, maple syrup, brown sugar and rum. Cook over low heat until mixture comes to a boil. Combine 2 tsp. of rum with 2 tsp. of cornstarch; slowly add to hot syrup mixture, stirring constantly until mixture thickens. Continue cooking 2-3 minutes.

Maple Indian Pudding

YIELD: 6 servings, PREP: 40 min, BAKE: 2½ hours

3 cups milk, scalded
1 cup cold milk
3 Tbsp. cornmeal
½ cup dark maple syrup
½ cup sugar
1 egg, beaten
½ tsp. salt
1 tsp. cinnamon
½ tsp. ginger
1 tsp. butter

Scald milk in a medium saucepan. Stir in cornmeal. Add maple syrup and cook until thick, stirring constantly. Remove from heat and add sugar, beaten egg, salt, cinnamon, ginger, and butter; mix well. Pour into buttered casserole dish and bake at 300°F for 30 minutes. Remove from oven and pour 1 cup cold milk over pudding. Return to oven and continue baking 2 more hours. Remove from oven and serve warm with *Maple Whipped Cream* (below).

Maple Whipped Cream

YIELD: 1½ cups, PREP: 10 min

¾ cup heavy cream
¼ cup maple syrup

Add heavy cream to a large bowl. With hand-held electric mixer, beat on high speed until stiff peaks form. Reduce speed on mixer to low and slowly drizzle in maple syrup until blended.

Maple Oatmeal Cookies

YIELD: 2 doz, PREP: 30 min, BAKE: 8-10 min

½ cup butter, softened
1 cup dark maple syrup
1 egg
1½ cups flour
1 tsp. baking powder
1 tsp. baking soda
1½ cups oatmeal
½ cup milk
½ cup walnuts, chopped
½ cup raisins

Beat butter, syrup, and egg. Add remaining ingredients, mixing well. Using medium scoop, drop onto greased cookie sheet. Bake at 350°F for 8 to 10 minutes. Cool on cookie sheet 5 minutes and then remove to cooling rack.

Maple Walnut Cookies

YIELD: 2½ doz cookies, PREP: 30 min, BAKE: 12 min

½ cup granulated maple sugar
½ cup brown sugar, packed
½ cup butter
½ cup sour cream
1 egg
½ tsp. natural maple flavoring*
2 cups flour
½ tsp. baking powder
½ tsp. baking soda
½ tsp. salt
1 cup walnuts, chopped

In large mixing bowl combine sugars, butter, sour cream, egg, and maple flavoring. With a handheld electric mixer beat on medium speed until creamy. Reduce speed and add dry ingredients; mix well. Stir in walnuts.

Using medium scoop, drop dough onto ungreased cookie sheets. Bake at 375°F for 10 to 13 minutes or until golden brown. When cool, frost with *Maple Cream Frosting* (below).

*Refer to page ix.

Maple Cream Frosting

YIELD: 1½ cups, PREP: 5-8 min

2 cups confectioners' sugar
4 Tbsp. butter, softened
⅓ cup maple syrup
½ cup walnuts, chopped
  (for decoration)

In medium bowl, combine confectioners' sugar and butter. Beat with hand-held electric mixer on low speed while gradually adding syrup until desired consistency. Spread on your favorite cake or cookie, such as *Maple Walnut Cookies* (above). Decorate with chopped walnuts.

Maple Icebox Cookies

YIELD: 3 doz, PREP: 30 min, BAKE: 12 min

½ cup butter, softened
1 egg
1 cup dark maple syrup
½ tsp. vanilla
3½ cups flour
½ tsp. baking soda
½ tsp. baking powder
¼ tsp. salt
½ cup walnuts, finely chopped

Beat butter, egg, syrup, and vanilla. Add flour, baking soda, baking powder, and salt. Mix well. Stir in nuts. Shape into two logs, wrap in plastic, and refrigerate 2 hours. Slice ¼ inch thick and place on lightly greased cookie sheet. Bake at 350°F for 12 minutes.

One of the recipes that I presented on the TV show "Across the Fence."

Coconut Maple Cookies

YIELD: 2 doz cookies, PREP: 20 min, BAKE: 12 min

½ cup maple sugar
½ cup white sugar
½ cup butter, softened
½ cup maple syrup
1 egg
½ tsp. vanilla
1½ cup flour
2 tsp. baking powder
½ tsp. salt
1 cup shredded coconut
1 cup walnuts, chopped

In a large bowl, cream sugars, butter, maple syrup, egg, and vanilla. Add flour, baking powder, and salt; mix well. Stir in coconut and walnuts.

Drop by medium scoop onto greased baking sheet. Bake at 350°F for 12 minutes until light brown.

Coconut Maple Macaroons

YIELD: 2 doz cookies, PREP: 15 min, BAKE: 15 min

2 eggs
½ cup butter, softened
1 cup maple syrup
½ cup milk
3 cups flour
½ tsp. salt
4 tsp. baking powder
1 cup shredded coconut

In mixing bowl, beat eggs and butter until light and fluffy. Add syrup and milk. Mix in dry ingredients. Drop by tablespoons onto greased baking sheet. Bake at 350°F for 15 minutes. Remove from oven and rest 2 minutes before removing to cooling rack.

Maple Custard

YIELD: 6 servings, PREP: 20 min, BAKE: 50 min

6 Tbsp. maple syrup
4 eggs
¼ cup maple syrup
½ tsp. salt
2 cups milk
¼ tsp. nutmeg

Spray 6 custard cups with nonstick spray. To each cup add 1 tablespoon of maple syrup. In large bowl beat eggs with maple syrup and salt. In medium saucepan, scald milk. While beating eggs, slowly pour in scalded milk. Pour into prepared custard cups and top each with a sprinkle of nutmeg. Set cups in pan of hot water and cook 50 minutes at 350°F or until knife inserted in center comes out clean.

Easy Maple Cream Tart

YIELD: 8 servings, PREP: 40 min plus chilling, BAKE: 15 min

2 cups pretzels, crushed
½ cup brown sugar, packed
6 Tbsp. butter, melted
1 can sweetened condensed milk
    (14 oz.)
⅔ cup maple syrup
¼ tsp. salt
1 cup heavy cream
¼ cup confectioners' sugar
1 tsp. vanilla

In medium bowl add crushed pretzels, brown sugar, and melted butter. Press evenly over the bottom and up sides of a 9" tart pan with removable bottom. Bake at 350°F for 15 minutes. Remove from oven and cool.

In top of double boiler, combine milk, syrup, and salt. Cook over boiling water until mixture bubbles, stirring occasionally. Cook 4 minutes. Pour into tart pan and cool 3 hours. In a large bowl, beat with hand-held electric mixer on high speed the cream, confectioners' sugar, and vanilla until stiff peaks form. Spread on tart and chill until ready to serve.

Maple Crème Brûlée

YIELD: 4 servings, PREP: 20 min plus chilling, BAKE: 50 min

½ cup maple syrup
3 egg yolks
1 egg
1 can evaporated milk (12 oz.)
½ cup milk
3 tsp. white sugar (approx.)

In a large bowl, beat eggs and add maple syrup to blend. Scald milk by heating in a small saucepan until a skim forms on the surface. While beating, slowly add hot milk mixture into egg mixture. Fill custard cups ¾ full. Set dishes into a 9" x 13" baking pan and add water to the halfway mark on the custard cups. Bake at 350°F until custard is set in the middle, 50 minutes.

Remove cups from pan and chill 4 hours, uncovered, until cold. Before serving, top with white sugar just enough to cover the surface. Caramelize and melt the sugar with a small torch until sugar is melted. Refrigerate to set before serving. Custard cups can also be placed under the broiler until sugar melts, about 1-2 minutes, being careful not to burn the sugar.

Maple Cream Pudding

YIELD: 8 servings, PREP: 20 min plus chilling

2 eggs, separated
¾ cup dark maple syrup
2 Tbsp. cornstarch
2 cups milk
¼ tsp. salt
1 tsp. vanilla

Separate eggs. Beat egg yolks. Place in top of double boiler the egg yolks, maple syrup, cornstarch, milk, and salt. Cook until thick, stirring constantly. Remove from heat, add vanilla, and cool. Whip egg whites with a dash of cream of tarter until thick. Fold into maple mixture. Chill until cool.

Maple Rice Pudding

YIELD: 8 servings, PREP: 15 min, BAKE: 30-40 min

2 cups prepared rice
(not instant rice)
2 cups milk
3 eggs, beaten
1 cup maple syrup
½ tsp. salt
¼ tsp. nutmeg
½ cup raisins

Scald milk in a small saucepan. In a medium mixing bowl, beat eggs, maple syrup, salt, and nutmeg. Slowly pour scalded milk into egg mixture while beating. Add raisins and cooked rice; mix to blend. Pour into small casserole dish and sprinkle with nutmeg. Place into a baking pan half-filled with water. Bake at 350°F for 30-40 minutes or until a knife inserted in the center comes out clean.

Biscuits & Syrup

YIELD: 9 servings, PREP: 25 min, BAKE: 30 min

2 cups flour
1 Tbsp. baking powder
⅓ cup shortening
½ tsp. salt
¾ cup milk

In a large bowl combine flour, baking powder, and salt. Add shortening and cut in until it reaches a mealy consistency. Add milk and mix until moistened. Form into a ball while in the bowl, remove, and place on a floured surface. Roll ½-¾ inches thick and cut out with biscuit cutter.

Put about 1½ inches of maple syrup into an 8-inch square pan. Top with baking powder biscuits. Bake at 375°F until biscuits are done, about 30 minutes.

This was one of my grandmother's favorite recipes. Simple and easy to make.

Fluffy Maple Tapioca

YIELD: 12 servings, PREP: 20 min plus cooling

4 egg whites
4 egg yolks, beaten
¼ tsp. cream of tarter
½ cup granulated maple sugar
7 Tbsp. Minute Tapioca
4 cups milk
1 tsp. vanilla

In medium bowl with electric mixer on high speed, beat egg whites with cream of tarter until foamy. Gradually add half of the granulated maple sugar (¼ cup), beating until soft peaks form.

Mix tapioca, milk, remaining ¼ cup of maple sugar, and beaten egg yolks in medium saucepan. Let stand 5 minutes. Cook on medium heat, stirring constantly, until mixture comes to a full boil. Remove from heat and add vanilla.

Quickly add to egg white mixture, folding until well blended. Cool 15 minutes. Serve warm or chilled.

Blonde Brownies

YIELD: 9 servings, PREP: 15 min, BAKE: 25 min

1 cup flour
¼ tsp. salt
½ tsp. baking powder
¼ tsp. baking soda
⅓ cup butter, melted
1 cup brown sugar, packed
1 egg, beaten
1 Tbsp. vanilla
½ cup white chocolate chips
½ cup walnuts, chopped

Butter a 9" x 9" baking pan. Combine the dry ingredients in a large mixing bowl. In a small microwave-safe bowl, melt butter, and add the brown sugar. Mix in the beaten egg and vanilla. Add to flour mixture, mixing well.

Stir in white chocolate chips and walnuts. Spread batter into baking pan. Bake at 350°F for 25 minutes. Serve with vanilla ice cream and *Salted Maple Walnut Sauce* (below).

Salted Maple Walnut Sauce

YIELD: 1 cup, PREP: 5 min, COOK: 10 min

½ cup maple sugar
¼ cup butter
¾ cup heavy cream
¼ cup walnuts, chopped
¼ tsp. sea salt

In small saucepan, cook the syrup and butter over low heat until thick. Slowly stir in cream and bring to a boil, stirring constantly until mixture coats a metal spoon. Mix in the walnuts and sea salt.

Spread on your favorite cake or ice cream, such as the *Blonde Brownies* (above).

Maple Whoopie Pies

YIELD: 7 pies, PREP: 15 min, BAKE: 20 min

 6 Tbsp. butter, softened
 1 egg
 ¾ cup sugar
 ½ cup maple syrup
 ¼ cup milk
 ½ tsp. natural maple flavoring*
2¼ cups flour
 1 tsp. baking powder
 1 tsp. salt
 ½ cup walnuts, chopped
     (optional)

 *Refer to page ix.

Cream together butter, egg, and sugar. Mix in syrup, milk, and maple flavoring. Beat in dry ingredients, mixing well. Drop by large scoop onto greased baking sheet. Bake at 375°F for approximately 20 minutes. Cool. Fill with *Maple Cream Cheese Spread* (page 11).

Maple Pretzel Bars

YIELD: 18 servings, PREP: 40 min, BAKE: 10 min

Bottom Crust:
- 2 cups pretzels, crushed
- ¾ cup butter, melted
- 3 Tbsp. white sugar

Second Layer:
- 3 eggs
- ½ cup water
- ⅔ cup flour
- 3 cups maple syrup
- 1 Tbsp. butter

Third Layer:
- 1 cup confectioners' sugar
- 8 oz. cream cheese, softened
- 1 cup whipped topping

In a large bowl, stir together crushed pretzels, melted butter, and sugar. Mix well and press into bottom of a 9" x 13" baking pan. Bake at 350°F for 10 minutes. Cool completely.

In a medium bowl, beat eggs, water, and flour. In a heavy-bottomed saucepan, whisk together syrup and egg mixture. Cook until mixture boils, stirring constantly to prevent scorching. Remove from heat and add butter. When cool, spread on crust.

In a medium bowl, beat all third-layer ingredients together. Spread over cooled second layer and garnish with chopped *Candied Maple Walnuts* (page 75).

Maple Ice Cream Sauce

YIELD: 2 cups, PREP: 5 min, COOK: 15 min

- 1¼ cups maple syrup
- 1 cup white sugar
- ½ cup heavy cream
- 2 Tbsp. maple liquor
- ½ cup walnuts, chopped

Combine maple syrup, sugar, cream, and liquor in a heavy saucepan. Bring mixture to a boil, stirring continuously. Reduce heat to low and cook for 5 minutes, stirring occasionally. Remove from heat, add walnuts, and cool.

Stir before using. Serve warm over ice cream. Refrigerate any leftover sauce.

Candied Maple Walnuts and Mom's Maple Fudge with Maple Sugar Candy (page 76)

Candy

Candied Maple Walnuts

YIELD: 4 cups, PREP: 15 min, BAKE: 10 min

4 cups walnut halves
2 cups maple syrup

Bring syrup to a boil. Add walnuts. Boil 8 minutes. Remove walnuts from syrup with a slotted spoon and transfer to a very lightly sprayed cookie sheet. Separate walnuts. Place in a 300°F oven for 10 minutes or until walnuts are bubbly. Remove at once from cookie sheet and cool. Keep in an airtight container.

Candied maple walnuts are great chopped and served as a garnish on your favorite salad.

Mom's Maple Fudge

YIELD: 1 lb, PREP: 10 min plus 45 min cooling, COOK: 1 hour

2 cups maple syrup
1 Tbsp. light corn syrup
¼ tsp. salt
½ cup milk
¼ cup cream
½ cup walnuts, chopped

In a medium saucepan, combine syrup, milk, cream, and salt. Attach candy thermometer, and cook without stirring to 236°F. Remove from heat and cool to 110°F, without stirring. Remove thermometer. Beat with a mixer or by hand until fudge loses its gloss. Add nuts and pour into buttered pan. Makes about 1 pound.

A friend gave this recipe to Mom and she entered it in a competition at the Vermont Farm Show, where it was a blue ribbon winner. The very best maple fudge I have ever eaten!

Maple Sugar Candy

YIELD: 2 cups, PREP: 5 min, COOK: 50 min

2 cups dark maple syrup
1 tsp. butter (for coating pot)

Pour syrup into a large heavy saucepan and butter sides; set over high heat. Clip a candy thermometer to the side of the pan; don't stir.

Cook to 238°F and remove from heat. Stir the mixture until it changes to a grainy consistency and lighter in color, five to 10 minutes. Pour the mixture into candy molds and let cool.

Maple Taffy

YIELD: 2 lbs, PREP: 10 min, COOK: 30 min

2 cups maple syrup
1 cup white sugar
¼ tsp. baking soda
1 Tbsp. butter

Butter a medium-size rimmed pan. Set aside. In a heavy-bottomed pan, combine syrup, sugar, baking soda, and butter. Boil all ingredients together until 295°F on a candy thermometer, or brittle when dropped in cold water.

Remove from heat and pour without scraping onto buttered pan. When cool enough to handle, pull and cut into 1-inch pieces.

Mixed-Nut Maple Brittle

YIELD: 1 lb, PREP: 5 min, COOK: 45 min

4 cups maple syrup
1 tsp. butter (for coating pot)
1 can mixed nuts (10 oz.)

In a medium heavy-bottomed saucepan, add syrup and insert candy thermometer. Bring to a boil and cook until 300°F on the candy thermometer. While cooking syrup, prepare a large rimmed baking pan. Cover with aluminum foil and spray lightly with cooking spray. Lay salted mixed nuts on foil. When syrup has reached 300°F, remove from heat and quickly pour over nuts. Cool and break into serving pieces.

I was making granulated maple sugar, which should only be cooked to 265°F, and wasn't paying attention. When I checked the syrup, it was already at 300°F. I quickly laid down some foil on a rimmed baking pan, sprayed it, dumped a can of mixed nuts on the foil and poured the syrup on top. After cooling, I had Mixed Nut Maple Brittle. It turned out very good: salty and sweet.

Chocolate-Dipped Maple Caramels

YIELD: 5 doz, PREP: 30 min plus 8 hours for cooling, COOK: 25 min

1 cup granulated maple sugar
1 cup dark corn syrup
1 cup butter
1 can sweetened condensed milk
  (14 oz.)
1 tsp. natural maple flavoring*
2 cups semisweet chocolate chips
2 Tbsp. shortening
1 Tbsp. Kosher salt (approx.)

*Refer to page ix.

These make a nice gift!

Prepare an 8" square pan by lining with aluminum foil and buttering bottom and sides. In a medium, heavy-bottomed saucepan, combine maple sugar, corn syrup, and butter. Bring to a boil without stirring and cook 7 minutes. Remove from heat and stir in condensed milk. Insert candy thermometer and return to medium heat. While stirring constantly to prevent scorching, bring to a boil and cook until 240°F on your candy thermometer, about 25 minutes. Remove from heat and stir in maple flavoring. Pour into prepared pan and let rest at room temperature 8 hours.

On a cutting board, invert caramel and remove foil. Cut into 1" squares. Line a rimmed pan with wax paper; set aside. Meanwhile, place chocolate chips and shortening into the top of a double boiler and place over hot water. Melt until smooth and combined. Turn off heat. Drop caramels into melted chocolate and turn until coated. With a fork remove caramels to lined pan. Sprinkle with Kosher salt. Place into mini cupcake wrappers.

Date Coconut Balls

YIELD: 24 balls, PREP: 10 min plus 15 min forming balls, COOK: 10 min

1 egg, beaten
½ cup butter
2 cups dates, chopped
1 cup granulated maple sugar
2 cups crisped rice cereal
½ cup walnuts, chopped
2 cups shredded coconut

In medium saucepan, combine beaten egg, butter, dates, and maple sugar. Cook over medium heat 10 minutes or until thick, stirring constantly to prevent scorching.

Remove from heat and pour over crisped rice cereal, mixing well. Add walnuts and mix in. Cool slightly.

Butter hands and form mixture into 1½-inch balls; roll in coconut. Place in air-tight container and chill in refrigerator.

Maple Lollipops

YIELD: 25 small lollipops, PREP: 7 min, COOK: 30 min

1 cup dark maple syrup
1 cup corn syrup
1 cup white sugar

Prepare lollipop molds by lightly spraying with a cooking spray; insert lollipop sticks. Combine in medium heavy-duty saucepan the maple syrup, corn syrup, and white sugar; insert candy thermometer. Heat to the hard crack stage (300°F). Reduce heat if the syrup starts to boil over.

Once it reaches 300°F, remove from heat and transfer the thermometer and syrup to a spouted glass measuring cup capable of withstanding a high temperature. Let the syrup cool to 270 degrees. Immediately pour into prepared molds. Let cool to room temperature. Remove the lollipops from the molds, place in bags and tie with a pretty ribbon or string.

Maple leaf lollipop molds must be made of material that will withstand high temperatures. I purchased mine from Leader Evaporator, a manufacturer of maple sugar equipment and supplies for over a century. For more information, see page ix.

Maple Divinity

YIELD: 2 doz, PREP: 20 min, COOK: 10 min

2 cups maple syrup
1 tsp. butter
2 egg whites
¼ tsp. salt
1 cup walnuts, chopped

In a 3-quart saucepan, place maple syrup and butter. Over high heat, boil to 260°F on a candy thermometer. Beat egg whites and salt until stiff peaks form. Slowly pour hot syrup over egg whites while beating.

Continue beating until soft peaks form and mixture starts to lose its gloss. Quickly add walnuts and drop by medium scoop onto waxed paper.

Divinity should be made only on a dry day. Humidity will affect the end result.

Maple Popcorn

YIELD: 4 quarts, PREP: 10 min, COOK: 30 min

½ cup popcorn
2 cups maple syrup
1 tsp. butter (for coating pan)

Cook syrup in a medium pan with inserted candy thermometer; butter sides of pan to prevent boil over. Cook to 245°F.

Pop popcorn and remove un-popped kernels. Place in a large buttered bowl.

Remove syrup from heat and stir until it begins to look cloudy. Pour immediately over popcorn and stir until cool and dry.

Notes

Notes

Notes

....

....

....

....

....

....

....

....

....

....

....

....

....

....

....

....

....

....

....

....

....

....

....

Notes

Index

27810204R00059

Made in the USA
Charleston, SC
24 March 2014